Scars That Heal
A Life Healed From the Inside Out

Written by Shannon Pope

ISBN: 1478358297
ISBN-13: 978-1478358299

Dear Ramie —

Here's to our Savior who completely restores, no band-aids!

♡ Always,

Shannon

DEDICATION

This book is dedicated to all my sisters. Those sisters in our congregation, those I meet across the United States and those I meet in countries across the globe – all with scars. May the transparency of my story and the word of my testimony give each and every one of you the courage to allow the cleansing of the Word of God and the salve of the Holy Spirit to begin the restoration process. Let His Words and the comfort of the Holy Spirit reach the tender and painful hurts. He always heals from the inside out. And He promises to heal everything that hurts you.

He promises to make something truly beautiful out of our mess.

ACKNOWLEDGMENTS

First and foremost, I would like to thank my Lord and Savior, Jesus Christ. Thank you for loving me enough to not only die on the cross for my sins, but to become bruised for all my iniquities. You, Lord Jesus, were bruised for every single one of them.

Thank you to my parents for raising me to know the Lord. Thank you to my loving husband, who truly is a real life example of Jesus' forgiving power. Thank you to my sons who teach me so much of what it really means to listen to the still small voice of the Holy Spirit. Thank you to my god daughter who taught me how to love in a broader way. Thank you to my sister who gives so much of her time to editing my mistakes without making fun of my challenges. Thank you to my brother for his kindness. Thank you to the endless list of friends who gave insight and direction to my personal writing.

CONTENTS

FORWARD

By Chris Pope, author's husband

In 1991 my life was turned up-side-down by a beautiful, intelligent, vivacious girl who was way out of my league. Her name was Shannon and somehow she would fall in love with this nerdy, awkward college boy and not long after become my wife.

As of the writing of this book we have been married eighteen years and I have never been more proud of her. In the pages that follow Shannon pours out the story of her life, a life that has undergone healing and transformation that can only come from God. The honesty and transparency of her writing make *Scars That Heal* a powerful and compelling read. I cannot begin to describe the overwhelming flood of emotions that overtook me as I read through this book for the first time. As husband and wife, Shannon and I are one. Her story is my story as well. As you will see, this story is not always pretty, sometimes painful, and always unabashedly truthful.

If you are hurting I pray this book helps you to find healing. If you have been brought out of brokenness into new life I pray that this book helps to embolden you to share what God has brought you through. It is a powerful thing when you share your story of Jesus in you. In fact Revelation 12:11 states "They overcame him by the blood of the lamb and by the word of their testimony; they did not love their lives so much as to shrink from death." You never know whose life will be changed when you tell your story of what Jesus has done in you and through you!

It is for this reason that Shannon has my full blessing to share our story. We are called to be over comers and this will only happen through the blood of Jesus Christ and the word of our (yours and mine) testimony.

INTRODUCTION

By Pastor Daniel Fitzpatrick, author's father

With no intent to impress religious leaders, Pastor Shannon Pope chose to instead Honor God and Serve Others. The latter identifies the purpose and thrust of her ordination. The purity, passion and perfection of the very heart of God's Great Commandment flows in this brief love offering as if it were the proverbial honey from God's personal honeycomb .

Born into the Kingdom as a called and ordained bond servant of the Word, she deliberately demonstrates that not unlike King David... She is indeed an anointed one after God's own heart. This jumps off the pages and into the reader's spirit, while saturating the soul and satiating the body as one realizes that the tears of remembrance brought by the realistic story telling has ushered one into that holy place. As Shannon seeks desperately the height, depth, and breadth of God's divine influence to affect self and others via Romans 12:2, I leave you with four R's:

READ with expectation of receiving from the throne of grace.
REFRESH yourself in the knowledge of God's mercy being offered fresh and new each morning.
RENEW your heart with a commitment to totally surrender to the Lord of Glory.
RESTORED by repetition of God's method of living in you through the renewal of your mind.

After all , the DNA of your intended father - before the foundations of the world - was to display and write on your heart His good pleasure ... To Give You The Kingdom...

MARKED FOR WHAT?

Daniel, by Elton John and lyricist Bernie Taupin, has always been a song I've been drawn to, not so much for the musical score, but more because I actually have a brother named Daniel. I used to tweak the wording a bit, and sing it to my "younger" brother when we were growing up. The song is a sad one though, and speaks of the brother's "scars that won't heal"[1].

We all have pain and scars, and I got to thinking about my own. Some pains have left actual physical scars, like the one on my left leg from when I was ten, and I decided I was old enough to shave my legs. I took off a three inch portion of my skin. Thirty years later, that scar still exists. There was pain at the time, but it doesn't hurt now. It's just a little ugly, and doesn't tan as well as the rest of me. The memory of the incident that caused the scar doesn't hurt either.

Then there are other scars that aren't physical, but emotional. There are memories stuck in our minds, some of the pain we have caused others, and some of the pain others have caused us. Both types of scars are tender and painful, and both can do significant damage if left untreated. This book is not about the "the pain from the scars that won't heal," but a collection of personal stories and revelation from the Holy Spirit about deep wounds and bruises that, when brought to the Light, can not only be healed, but can actually be transformed.

Romans 12:1-2, *"Therefore, I urge you, brothers and sisters, in view of God's mercy, to offer your bodies as a living sacrifice, holy and pleasing to God—this is your true and proper worship. Do not conform to the pattern of this world, but be transformed by the renewing of your mind. Then you will be able to test and approve what God's will is —his good, pleasing and perfect will."*

When I was in first grade, my next door neighbor became my permanent substitute teacher when the regular teacher fell ill. This was a big deal for me: one, because I was now the class favorite, and two, because I got to help with the butterflies. Our class had a butterfly project, and we would watch the Painted Lady caterpillars transform day to day. The smell of the tank is still stuck in my memory as it was a distinct scent from the sugar/vitamin water that the caterpillars sipped. The caterpillar would become wrapped in the chrysalis, and then after seven to ten days, would transform into a new creature, a butterfly. I loved helping with this! Years later, I would learn that this is exactly what God does for us. At our moment of conversion, he transforms us into a "new creation."

2 Corinthians 5:17 declares, *"If anyone is in Christ, he is a new creation; old things have passed away; behold, all things have become **new**."*

If you have made the decision and the confession (Romans 10:9-10) that Jesus is your Savior and the Lord of your life, you too have become a new creation. You may look the same, but you look different to God the Father. He sees you through the blood of Jesus, and your sins don't exist anymore. You are new and clean. This is really incredible news! The problem is that we are a tripartite person – simply said, we are made of three parts. The Spirit is *WHO* you really are, and this is the part that gets "saved" and becomes "new." The Soul is what you possess, and interestingly enough, your soul is also made up of three parts: your mind, your will and your emotions. (This book mainly addresses this part – "the renewing of your mind" – the soul.) The third part of you is your body, and this is the part that will stop working one day and die.

Most of the issues that I deal with as a pastor are issues regarding the soul – the mind, the will, and the emotions. The Bible speaks about renewing the mind by washing it with the Word of God. The Bible also talks about "working out your salvation." In Philippians 2:12-13 it says:

"Therefore, my dear friends, as you have always obeyed—not only in my presence, but now much more in my absence—continue to work out your salvation with fear and trembling, for it is God who works in you to will and to act in order to fulfill his good purpose."

This doesn't mean we keep on doing good deeds to work to earn our salvation. No Way! The Bible is very clear that salvation is a free gift, and there's nothing that can be done to earn it. We do good deeds and serve others *because* we are rescued by Christ, and because it gives God glory. "Working out your salvation" in my opinion has to do will this soul issue – the part of us that, though designed by God, got so messed up, it needs renewing.

So, I'm left with the challenge of writing things down for the world to see that, personally, I'd rather they not. But because I know my story might help someone else, I will give it my best shot. Some people would be quick to warn a person off from writing such a book. Too much information in the public light can be damaging to one's career, etc. But I choose to believe the words of a much greater influence, the Holy Spirit.

In Revelation 12:11 it states:

"They triumphed over him by the blood of the Lamb and by the word of their testimony; they did not love their lives so much as to shrink from death."

Since I am a firm believer that what the Bible says is true, I believe that we do overcome by Jesus' blood (what He did for us on the Cross), and by our own story. The Blood of the Lamb is something we have zero control over. He gives this cleansing of sin and sickness away freely through His blood. This is a free gift that we can either receive or reject. But, the Word of our testimony is something that we do have control over. It requires our active participation. In other Scripture, it tells us that "faith, by itself, if it not accompanied by action, is dead." Since I know that God told me to write this story down and make it available to others, I know I am applying the active participation to my faith.

God's Word tells us very specific things about ourselves. One of these key verses is found in Psalms 139: 13-19:

"Oh yes, you shaped me first inside, then out; you formed me in my mother's womb.
I thank you, High God—you're breathtaking! Body and soul, I am marvelously made!
I worship in adoration—what a creation!
You know me inside and out, you know every bone in my body;
You know exactly how I was made, bit by bit,
how I was sculpted from nothing into something.
Like an open book, you watched me grow from conception to birth;
all the stages of my life were spread out before you,
The days of my life all prepared before I'd even lived one day."

This text shows us some very important truths. One of those truths is *you and I are not mistakes.* This is great news! Another truth is *No matter how you were made; God formed you and thinks you are marvelous.* More great news! Then there's another truth that is revealed: *All of our days, even the yucky ones, are known to God.* That last one used to bother me. I know I make my own choices, but sometimes choices are made for us, and sometimes things are done to us that go against our own will. These things can leave an imprint.

My friend sent me to lyrics to this song, *Heal the Wound,* by Point of Grace.

I used to wish that I could rewrite history
I used to dream that each mistake could be erased
Then I could just pretend
I never knew the me back then

4

I used to pray that You would take this shame away
Hide all the evidence of who I've been
But it's the memory of
The place You brought me from
That keeps me on my knees
And even though I'm free

Heal the wound but leave the scar
A reminder of how merciful You are
I am broken, torn apart
Take the pieces of this heart
And heal the wound but leave the scar[2]

I've allowed God to heal many wounds for me. I am praying that through the reading of this book, you will allow Him to do the same for you. There are moments that mark you, that leave a big imprint on your soul. These imprints may show the path you've taken. There are also moments that mark you and define you. Those moments shape **who** you are. These moments define you, and lead to the purpose for which you are headed.

Jeremiah 29:11-13, *"For I know the plans I have for you," declares the* LORD, *"plans to prosper you and not to harm you, plans to give you hope and a future. Then you will call on me and come and pray to me, and I will listen to you. You will seek me and find me when you seek me with all your heart."*

This is a story of the marks that led to the defining moments in my life.

INNOCENCE STOLEN

Few people were as blessed as me growing up. I came from a nuclear family: married parents, a brother, a sister, a dog. My dad worked all the time, so we really only saw him on Sundays; most of the time it was just my siblings and my mom and I. Consistency in church attendance as a child is what I knew as normal. It's what you did, what good families did. And we were what most would consider a good family.

There were moments during my childhood when the spirit of God would come on me, and show me pictures. This may sound silly, but at one point my sister and I were active with a children's ministry that put on musicals for kids. This group gained some local notoriety, and we were invited to participate in a "road trip" where we performed this musical in five cities throughout the Midwest. During those moments on stage, as a dancer and singer, God would show me glimpses of being in front of others sharing the Gospel. The picture was different then the dancing stuff, and to be honest I didn't understand it, and didn't spend much time thinking about it. I just remember how fun the group was, and how I got to hang out with my friends during those times. Later God would show me what these "pictures" meant. Later, He would reveal to me that He was marking my future.

Remember Jeremiah 29:11 which says,

"For I know the plans I have for you," declares the LORD, "plans to prosper you and not to harm you, plans to give you hope and a future."

My parents were what some would call overprotective, and that began to really bother me when I became a teenager. I longed for the freedom most of my classmates and friends had. My obedient reputation and my ability to charm others put me in a favorable position to begin to manipulate my situation. Freedom from my loving, but overprotective parents was the goal, and cleverness was the tactic I used.

I had a new friend who fascinated me. She was uninhibited and daring. Aside from her carefree life, she was also a lot of fun to hang out with, and she introduced me to some things I had never experienced before: cigarettes, shoplifting - even a little pot smoking. The upside was she occasionally attended my church. She came from a broken family, so my friendship with her appeared like I was the role model Christian influencing the hurting teen. In actuality, the influencing came from her, and I couldn't have been happier about that. She even had an older brother, a good looking older brother with a great personality. He was not like the boys at my school or the ones in my youth group. Talking with him came easily. He had a great sense of humor, and he sure knew how to flirt. I had kissed a few boys already, but kissing him was different because he was older, more mature.

My mother was unaware of my relationship with my friend's brother. For some reason though, she refused to allow me to spend the night at my friend's house. This is what girls did back in the day – have sleepovers, so being denied a sleepover frustrated and angered me. My mom and I would have arguments over her refusal to my requests. I assumed her reasons regarded the divorced household and the fact that my friend's mother had lots of boyfriends in and out of the house. But, as I said, I was clever. I devised a plan for my friend and I to attend a Bible study at our youth pastor's house, and then afterward we would spend the night at my friend's grandparents' home. This plan was well received since the grandparents lived within walking distance from the pastor, and of course, the grandparents had been married for over 45 years. My friend and I were happy with our mastery over the protective parents and had a great night in store filled with all kinds of vices and pleasures.

When we arrived at her grandparents' house, we were greeted with pizza, soda, and rented movies. This was a big deal back then, and I'm sure this dates me, but few people I knew had VCRs, let alone the home theatre system these people owned. There was one more thing waiting for me at their house: the older brother! Apparently, he was much more clever than I could have ever been because he found out our plans and managed to work out an arrangement to spend the weekend at the grandparents' house. My heart raced at the thought of having a sleepover at the same house as the boy I had a crush on. The night went on, and after the first movie, the grandparents went to bed. Despite the stereo surround sound being so loud, my friend wound up falling asleep in the middle of the living room floor. There I was, in the middle of the night, fourteen years old, alone on the couch with a boy that was really into me. We were holding hands, and then we started kissing...really kissing. The volume blaring out of the speakers was painfully loud. I remember the movie playing was *Indiana Jones and the Temple of Doom*[3], and it was the part when the witch doctor pulls out the guy's heart. All of a sudden he was on top of me. I didn't want him on me. I called out for my friend. I screamed for her! She couldn't hear me. I screamed for her grandparents! They couldn't hear me. Then he pinned my arms above my head. He was a lot stronger than me, and I couldn't move. I turned my head, and saw the scene with the witch doctor holding up the heart. It all happened so fast, but in slow motion at the same time. No one could hear me fight him. I couldn't even hear me. No one could hear me scream. I felt like he was holding up my heart...taking my life. No one knew what was happening to me. I cried out to God! God didn't stop it from happening.

I never told anyone, and I managed to block it out my memory. At age fourteen that moment left an imprint on me.

CHOOSING LIFE, ETERNAL LIFE

I went on being the church attending, obedient girl, but clever and manipulative when it would suit me. That moment on the couch wasn't in my memory, but the imprint was definitely there. It would ultimately damage my decision making ability for years to come. I went along being a fairly happy teen. I had lots of friends, and I had a few non-serious relationships with boys. My home life was challenging. It felt like I lived in a single parent household most of the time. My parents were married, but I rarely saw my dad. He would leave for work before I would wake up for school, and he usually got home after I was already in bed at night. My mom seemed stressed out all the time. My sister and I helped out a lot with our baby brother and doing household chores. My one outlet was youth group at church. Most of my friends went there every week, so I looked forward to it.

One night, I was attending my youth group, and the pastor was speaking. I was sitting with all my girlfriends, and I felt a warm sensation. It was like there was a spotlight in that gymnasium, and a bright light shown directly from heaven, through the gym ceiling, and rested directly on my head. I wept. I saw my sin of my former manipulations and lies, and I cried out to God for forgiveness. The pastor had an altar call, and I ran up to rededicate my life to the Lord. I received the love God had for me, and I made a promise to God that I would follow Him. I also promised that, if I dated anyone else, it would be someone with a heart after Him. That moment marked me and would eventually shape me. It defined me as a child of the Most High God. My spirit was right with the Lord. I was His. This moment is when my spirit became "new" as we read in Second Corinthians.

This choice I made for Christ defined my status with Him. I knew my name was now written in the Lamb's Book of Life. I knew that when I would die, I would instantly be with my loving Savior in heaven. I knew this was the most important decision I would every make. A choice was set before me, and I knew I had chosen the right one.

Deuteronomy 30:11-20, *Now what I am commanding you today is not too difficult for you or beyond your reach. It is not up in heaven, so that you have to ask, "Who will ascend into heaven to get it and proclaim it to us so we may obey it?" Nor is it beyond the sea, so that you have to ask, "Who will cross the sea to get it and proclaim it to us so we may obey it?" No, the word is very near you; it is in your mouth and in your heart so you may obey it.*

See, I set before you today life and prosperity, death and destruction. For I command you today to love the LORD your God, to walk in obedience to him, and to keep his commands, decrees and laws; then you will live and increase, and the LORD your God will bless you in the land you are entering to possess.

But if your heart turns away and you are not obedient, and if you are drawn away to bow down to other gods and worship them, I declare to you this day that you will certainly be destroyed. You will not live long in the land you are crossing the Jordan to enter and possess.

This day I call the heavens and the earth as witnesses against you that I have set before you life and death, blessings and curses. **Now choose life***, so that you and your children may live and that you may love the LORD your God, listen to his voice, and hold fast to him. For the LORD is your life, and he will give you many years in the land he swore to give to your fathers, Abraham, Isaac and Jacob.*

This moment clearly was a defining one for me. I chose life. Defining moments are either good or bad, and they come with blessings or with curses. Now it was my time to live out this choice for life. It is clear that there were times coming up when I would not know how to live out this choice.

FIRST LOVE

A year went by, and I met a boy. Really, to me he was a man in a teenage body. I would watch him worship at youth group, and his passion for God captivated me. He was passionate about everything and was so easy to talk to. I really don't know how it happened, but we started talking a lot and shortly after we started "going out." We didn't attend the same school or live near each other, but that didn't matter. We found ways to be together. He pursued me, and I loved it! He would often take the bus to my house, and spend the day with me and my family. We became inseparable. Most of our activities together revolved around God or church. We had youth group retreats, home group meetings, youth group, and once we started driving, we were on weekly dates. He treated me with so much respect. I loved him. He loved me, and we both loved the Lord. It was perfect!

There was one problem: I couldn't keep my hands off him. He was gorgeous. Of course, as a teenage male, he returned the gestures, and it wasn't long before we had a more serious relationship. There would be times where our devotion to the Lord turned to a deep devotion towards each other. Instead of putting our relationship with God first, we would put each other first. I believe that our shifting of priorities, combined with teenage hormones, led to us becoming more intimate with each other. The Message paraphrase of the Book of James 1:13-15 says it this way, *"Don't let anyone under pressure to give in to evil say, 'God is trying to trip me up.' God is impervious to evil, and puts evil in no one's way. The temptation to give in to evil comes from us and only us. We have no one to blame but the leering, seducing flare-up of our own lust. Lust gets pregnant, and has a baby: sin! Sin grows up to adulthood, and becomes a real killer".*

The cleverness I once had came right back, and we'd come up with all kinds of creative ways to be alone. At first, I would feel guilty each time we had sex, and I'd find myself at the altar the next time we were at church repenting of my sin. Of course, the very next time we were together, we "were together."

Everywhere I was, I was being warned of the pitfalls of premarital sex: school, my parents, and even my youth group. I couldn't get away from the conviction. 1 Corinthians 6:16-20 (The Message) was one that rang through my ears, and would knock on the door of my heart.

*"There's more to **sex** than mere skin on skin. **Sex** is as much spiritual mystery as physical fact. As written in Scripture, "The two become one." Since we want to become spiritually one with the Master, we must not pursue the kind of **sex** that avoids commitment and intimacy, leaving us more lonely than ever—the kind of **sex** that can never "become one." There is a sense in which **sex**ual sins are different from all others. In **sex**ual sin we violate the sacredness of our own bodies, these bodies that were made for God-given and God-modeled love, for "becoming one" with another. Or didn't you realize that your body is a sacred place, the place of the Holy Spirit? Don't you see that you can't live however you please, squandering what God paid such a high price for? The physical part of you is not some piece of property belonging to the spiritual part of you. God owns the whole works. So let people see God in and through your body."*

 I heard this scripture repeated over and over in my mind.

The more and more I chose what felt right, the more and more I justified what I was doing and what we were doing as okay. The red flags and the warnings were shooting off all around me like a fireworks finale. The Word of God was convicting me in my sin, but my sin became more and more deliberate, and part of me stopped caring about the consequences. Eventually, I had no more guilt. We had made plans to get married after high school. I had some great high school years because of him and because we were head over heels with each other. But I also knew I was putting him first over my relationship with God.

Ezekiel 18:30 warns, *"I will judge each of you according to your own ways, declares the Sovereign LORD. **Repent**! Turn away from all your offenses; then sin will not be your downfall."*

I didn't repent. Then it happened, I don't know how, but it happened. Maybe it was because his family moved over an hour away. Maybe it was because I graduated high school, and he still had two more years to go. Maybe we just grew apart. But it happened. We broke up, and I was devastated! I fell into a deep depression, and I felt alone. My heart was ripped out. Was I being punished for my sin? I cried out to God. He didn't respond. A big imprint was left on my soul.

I did the next step of the typical eighteen year old high school graduate; I enrolled in college at the local university. I didn't really want to be in school, but I didn't know what else to do with myself. All my plans and hopes were lost. Giving so many years and so much of myself to my relationship with my boyfriend changed me. He had my soul – my mind, my will, and my emotions. Everything that should have been God's, I gave to him, and I felt empty and alone.

So I did the stupid thing and dated a couple guys. I didn't really like them, but it filled a temporary void. I never went more than a month without a date. I asked God to help me because I could feel myself starting to down spiral. I sought out my former youth pastor for counseling, and he spent a lot of time with me encouraging me and reminding me who I was in Christ. I knew God would hear my cries and help me. Little did I know, but His answer to my cries would come sooner than expected.

Psalm 28:2 states, "***Hear my cry*** *for mercy as I call to you for help, as I lift up my hands toward your Most Holy Place."*

TWO BECOMING ONE

I'm now a college student, living at home, attending a local commuter university. One day I was sitting in Freshman Composition at the university about ready to submit an essay assignment. I had written an essay on the "Most Influential Person in My Life." I wrote about my youth pastor - how time and time again, he was there for me despite my mistakes. My professor instructed the class to swap essays with another student and edit one another's essays. I swapped with the nerdy guy in front of me. He read my story, and I began to read his essay. I was amazed at how similar his essay was to my own. He wrote of his salvation experience at a youth retreat the year prior and the impact the leaders there had on his life. All of the sudden he didn't seem so dorky to me. We were inspired by each other's stories, and began to hang out every day before class.

The spark I had with my high school boyfriend wasn't there. We had something different. He was genuine, innocent, and pure. This appealed to me since I wasn't pure. I wanted a pure relationship. I admired him. The cleverness that had gotten me in so much trouble in the past didn't exist with him. I felt safe.

Psalm 23:3-5, *"Who may ascend the mountain of the Lord? Who may stand in his holy place? The one who has clean hands and a **pure heart**,* *who does not trust in an idol or swear by a false god. They will receive blessing from the LORD and vindication from God their Savior."*

Eventually, I found myself falling for this guy, who was totally not my type. He was shy, quiet and socially awkward at times. But I liked the simplicity and the genuineness of our friendship. We started attending church together, and he grew so much spiritually. He became a great role model for me in my obedience to the Scriptures. The things that took years for me to mature in seemed to happen to him overnight. I liked being around him.

After six months of dating, he gave me a promise ring. My sexual desires were strong, and before long I took his virginity. He was so convicted of our sin, he repented immediately. I felt horrible because my conviction didn't seem exist. I wondered how I had become so calloused to sex. I knew premarital sex was wrong, but I truly didn't care. It became a constant problem in our relationship.

We decided to switch majors and change colleges together, and we both moved a couple hours away from home to another city in our home state. He stayed in the dorms, and I stayed with a friend in an apartment. Our lives consisted of school, work, homework and working toward our future careers. Our schedules were demanding, and mine seemed to consume me. At one time I was taking 18 credit hours and working four part time jobs. My schedule didn't allow for much church attendance, and I didn't actively change my schedule to fit it in either.

Malachi 1:7 (The Message) warns, *When you say, 'The altar of God is not important anymore; worship of God is no longer a **priority**,' that's defiling.*

It wasn't long after getting settled in our new college town that my boyfriend proposed, and I accepted. Less than a year later we were married by my former youth pastor. I still had one year of school to go, and my new husband had another year and a half to go before he could graduate.

The fast pace of college life naturally morphed right into the fast pace of career life for me. I was moving up in management in my field, while my husband was struggling to find a job in his specific career path. He eventually applied for a position in another state, and was hired instantly. Before we knew it, we were leaving my employment security and everything behind, and we relocated 1100 miles from home.

Even though I was leaving my job, relocating was an adventure for us. We loved the new tropical climate, and explored all our new state had to offer. But despite the beauty of our new location, loneliness reared its ugly head for me. I had no prospects in my field. Here I was a college graduate with a high grade point average, and loads of work experience, but I couldn't find a job! I went from having a jam-packed weekly schedule to having absolutely nothing to do. My husband had to work two jobs to make our ends meet. I started resenting my husband for the move. I had no friends and no job, and I was bored and miserable. My husband didn't have much time for me with his demanding work schedule, and my mind began to wonder what life would have been like with my high school love. My husband's and my life together seemed passionless.

POSTPARTUM BLUES

Before long, I became pregnant. I never wanted to be pregnant, just adopt someday in the future, but this unexpected pregnancy made me excited that I would have someone to ease my loneliness. I would have someone all for myself. The boredom of my life wouldn't last long with a baby on the way. Preparations for the baby's arrival were cut short when a routine checkup at the doctor's turned into an emergency inducing delivery of the baby. I was totally caught off guard when my son was delivered, and he couldn't breathe. His premature birth demanded he be immediately placed on a breathing machine since his little lungs weren't fully developed. The doctors and nurses whisked him away, and before I even had a chance to hold my son, or even see what he looked like, he was being treated in the NICU. That moment was a defining moment in my life. It changed me. Again, I felt like my heart was ripped out my chest and someone was holding it. I felt completely empty.

I spent hours at his bedside in the NICU praying. His breathing was labored, and he took longer than most preemies to get better. I would spend at least five hours each day uncontrollably bawling. My mother flew in town to be with me, and she helped me get back and forth from the children's hospital. She would spend hours holding me, which was my only comfort as I was not allowed to hold my child.

Our son had many difficulties his first year of life. I was sleep deprived because of his challenges, and I most likely had a good case of undiagnosed postpartum depression, yet I refused to see a doctor. The loneliness I was trying to escape from didn't seem to want to leave, and my husband's work schedule and the new demands of motherhood just seemed to heighten my awareness of it.

When our son turned one, we had an opportunity to return home so my husband could have a chance to earn his master's degree. His new employer agreed to pay for his continued education which pleased us very much since additional student loans were no longer an option. This also made me happy since a graduate degree would enable him to earn a higher income, and he'd be able to quit working a second job, which meant more time for our little family. Relocating back home also meant my family and my friends, and bye-bye to the loneliness.

THE BITTER TASTE

I jumped into life back home without missing a beat. I signed up as a monthly volunteer at the church nursery, and started taking a Bible study class during the week. Things got awkward when I went to services weekly by myself. My husband worked night shifts as well as weekend shifts to get a higher pay differential, so he rarely was with me at church. Guys would often approach before and after church services, and ask me out on dates. I would say something like, "Don't you see this wedding ring on my finger and this toddler holding my hand?" Nevertheless, it was flattering; at the same time, it made me feel alone.

My husband delayed enrolling in the master's program that we had moved back home for. The next deadline for school approached, and I filled out the paperwork for him, leaving only his signature to finish the application. He didn't follow through with the enrollment. I was frustrated that his chance for advancement and our chance to have him work normal hours was farther and farther away in the picture. My irritation with all this turned into flat out resentfulness towards him.

I started coming up with ways to spend as much time with my husband as possible. To ensure he didn't have to do any chores on his day off, I would even go as far as to mow the lawn while my son was down for naps. I would attach the baby monitor to my hip and occasionally glance down to see if any red dots were showing on the monitor indicating if he was crying. I made sure everything was done in the house so I could spend as much time with him as possible when he was home. This backfired because his lack of responsibility at home freed him up to do things outside the home, and away from me and our son. He joined his brother's blues band as the drummer and spent most of his days off with the band. His new hobby infuriated me, causing me to plead my case to my husband, and sometimes even beg for a little attention. His argument was that he works really hard to provide for our family and he deserves to do something he loves. Of course this would turn into a regular argument as I just wanted time with him. I didn't have an opportunity to have a hobby, why should he? He was a good man, and deserved everything he was wanting, but I just wanted a husband who was present. I wanted to go to church as a family. As months of the same routine continued, I began to feel like a single mother with a roommate that slept during the days. Our marriage was crumbling. I wanted out. The resentment grew to bitterness. That bitterness started to make an imprint on me.

I would read scriptures like Ephesians 4:30-32, but I didn't know how to carry them out. *"And do not grieve the Holy Spirit of God, with whom you were sealed for the day of redemption. Get rid of all bitterness, rage and anger, brawling and slander, along with every form of malice. Be kind and compassionate to one another, forgiving each other, just as in Christ God forgave you."*

TEMPTATION TURNS HEADS

I reconnected with some old friends and would get a babysitter once a week so I could have some sort of social life. It was fun, but I also received a lot of attention from men while we were out. Instead of making me feel good, the attention made me feel sad because I was alone. I started to really resent my husband and the choices I had made: quitting my career, moving twice, having a baby. I didn't know what to do next. I found myself fantasizing about my old love, the one I was with for four years in high school. What if I had married him? Why didn't I? I started looking at our old photos. I even drove by the house he used to live in. My thinking became all messed up, and thoughts of him consumed me.

Romans 1:20-22, *"For since the creation of the world God's invisible qualities—his eternal power and divine nature—have been clearly seen, being understood from what has been made, so that people are without excuse. For although they knew God, they neither glorified him as God nor gave thanks to him, but their thinking became futile and their foolish hearts were darkened. Although they claimed to be wise, they became fools."*

It was Easter Sunday at church, and I was sitting next to my sister and a girlfriend. The church was packed as usual, worship had just ended, and everyone was seated. All of the sudden someone stood up in the front row, and walked down the aisle to the back lobby. My heart jumped up in my throat, and began to race. I exclaimed, "O my gosh...it's him!" I felt like I was having an anxiety attack. My heart was racing so fast! It felt like my heart was beating out of my chest. It was my ex! Why was I reacting like this? It has been over eight years since we had seen each other, and I had been married five of those years. I searched for him unsuccessfully after the service, and each Sunday that followed. Was God bringing him back to me so we could have a second chance together?

My memories of my ex consumed me. I didn't know at the time how he got my number, but he ended up calling me. I found out he had been thinking of me too, and even used a people finder agency to track me down. This was pre-Facebook, so finding people was a little more challenging. It felt like the best conversation I had ever had. Just minutes on the phone with him was more exhilarating than the last year of my relationship with my spouse. I was thrilled! It felt great to reconnect with him, and I immediately told my husband of my conversation. His response was not what I expected. He said, "It's great you two can be friends after all these years." What? Friends? I wanted a lot more than to just be friends. Couldn't he see that?

Our phone conversations continued, my heart racing each time I'd hear his voice. I would feel guilty about my feelings, and I would try to create magical moments with my husband when he was home from work. The feelings didn't register on the same scale. I continued to be forthright with my husband about my phone calls and my feelings. I was disappointed all the more with my marriage when my friendship with my ex didn't seem to bother my husband at all. I really wanted out of my marriage. I felt like he didn't even care. His complacency marked me.

Proverbs 1:32, *"For the waywardness of the simple will kill them, and the complacency of fools will destroy them."*

I also knew my desires were wrong. Mark 4:18-19 warns about desires for other things choking the word, *"Still others, like seed sown among thorns, hear the word; but the worries of this life, the deceitfulness of wealth and the desires for other things come in and choke the word, making it unfruitful."* It was like I knew what was happening, but instead of trusting God to help me, I was giving into those desires.

My ex wanted me back, and I wanted him. Memories of our former sexual encounters played like a movie in my head. I would lay awake at night replaying the same movie over and over. Eventually talking on the phone wasn't enough for me. I wanted to see him, and I arranged to meet him at his place. I was so nervous driving over there. I couldn't get there fast enough. I melted inside when he opened the door. Everything about him felt so right. We talked for hours, and eventually he asked if he could kiss me. I shook my head yes. We kissed, but inside I wanted to do more.

Our phone calls got more intimate, and we started making plans for a future. I couldn't wrap my head around how I could get divorced and still be a Christian. I knew God's Word said that God hates divorce and only gave a couple of reasons to allow it. Of course my marriage didn't reflect those reasons. My weekly Bible study was even talking about temptation and the rewards that come from being obedient to God. I felt like scum because I was giving in to my feelings. I truly wanted what was tempting me. I ended up confiding in my mom about my feelings for my ex, and how I wasn't in love with my husband anymore. She held me and listened while I cried in her lap for hours.

SAYING THE "D" WORD

I had gotten really sick with a double ear infection and fever, and the antibiotics prescribed weren't clearing it up. It was difficult to care for my son while being sick, especially since my husband worked nights and slept during the days, so my parents kept my son for a couple days. One of those evenings, I invited my ex over. I was feeling so awful, and I just wanted to be taken care of. It was awkward when he came in my home, and he saw our family photos. Everything felt more real, and the prospect of divorce became clearer to me; I knew that none of this would be easy. We didn't give in to temptation that evening, but we did talk and kiss, and it was wonderful. He gave me hope that my future wouldn't remain in this stagnant state.

I became increasingly transparent with my husband, and finally got a reaction out of him when I told him that I loved talking to my ex on the phone and how great he makes me feel. He asked me if we needed to go talk to someone about our marriage. I said, "how about you talk to me, and spend time with me first?" I asked him to stay home from work that night, and when he walked out the door, it felt like he didn't value me at all.

I decided to make plans to secure my future financially. I got re-hired as a part time manager at a former place of employment, and I negotiated full time benefits, so I could ensure health insurance for myself. I bought a car in my name, so I would have transportation in the event of divorce. I found an old friend who said I could live with her. Things were practically falling into place.

I couldn't stand it anymore. I resented my marriage more than ever. I felt trapped in a love-less relationship. I knew I wanted out, so I decided to do the one thing that would cause my husband to leave me. I drove over to my boyfriend's house with every intention of having sex with him. We did. I didn't feel guilty at all.

The next day when my husband woke up, I told him right away. He had never been one to be emotional, but with tears in his eyes he punched a hole in the wall, and dented in the back door. I was trembling in fear. I grabbed our son and rushed him over to our neighbor's house. When I came back, my husband began asking details that I refused to give. I told him I wanted a divorce. Through his tears, he said no. Then he said something I never expected. He said, "I will forgive you for this!" What? Forgive me? That wasn't the plan! That's not what I wanted at all. I wanted out! I wanted to make a life with the one who was passionate about me, who really desired me, who completed me. I didn't want to be forgiven.

TO OBEY IS BETTER THAN SACRIFICE

Things sure didn't go as I had planned. I stopped talking to my husband all together. I didn't feel bad for what I did against my husband, but the truth of my choice affected my relationship with God. I knew I hurt Him. I continued to go to church. I was leaving the service one Sunday, and I bumped into my former youth pastor. Bumping into someone I knew wasn't always common as thousands of people attended each service. He immediately knew there was something wrong with me. I blurted everything out, and told him what I did. I told him I wanted a divorce, and I was going to have a life with my boyfriend. He replied, "You're not doing anything until we talk!" I said "well let's talk now 'cause this is what I'm going to do." He told me a bit of truth, and gave me a stern warning. I was upset, but knew he was speaking from the heart. He loved me. On the way home, I was searching for a cassette to play in my car. I was driving down the highway so I really couldn't pay attention to what I was grabbing, and popped in the first cassette tape I could reach. An old song began to play - a song I hadn't heard in years. "To Obey is Better than Sacrifice" by Keith Green[4]. Of all tapes, I grabbed the one that was word for word Scriptures! The lyrics brought tears to my eyes. I knew I was probably taking the words out of context, but to me staying in my love-less marriage was a sacrifice, but obeying God was so much better. I knew God wanted my obedience. Could I really do something He hates? Or, could I stay in the marriage and obey

Him? It seemed impossible.

1 Samuel 15:22, "*But Samuel replied: 'Does the LORD delight in burnt offerings and sacrifices as much as in obeying the LORD? To obey is better than sacrifice, and to heed is better than the fat of rams.'*"

Something prevented me from taking my son and physically moving out of the house. I had everything packed, but each time I tried to move, I couldn't do it. It's like my muscles wouldn't work, and I couldn't physically move. My husband started leaving me notes around the house - love notes. I hated reading them. I couldn't believe he was writing to me in this way after what I did to him. It made me feel worse about myself. One morning I woke up, and there was an amethyst ring on my finger – my favorite gem stone. I also noticed he was reading the Bible. I hadn't seen him do that for years.

My boyfriend stopped taking my calls. Apparently my husband contacted him, and told him never to contact me again. I was so upset with both of them – my husband for doing that, and my boyfriend for giving in to his request.

Eventually, my husband and I started talking to each other, mostly about our son. He quit the band, and would invite me out on dates, and even family dates. I didn't know what to say to him when we were together, but he kept pursuing me. I really didn't remember him ever pursuing me in the beginning of our relationship together, but now he was really after me.

Shortly after the rebuilding of our relationship took on a solid momentum, I signed up for a short term mission trip with our church. I knew I needed to take an action, and turn away from my mistakes, and serve the Lord somehow. With my husband's blessing, I left my husband and son for eight days, and served alongside many sold-out servants of Christ in a warehouse that prepared gifts for children. The impact of these gifts reached millions throughout the globe, and this simple mission reignited a passion that burned in me as a child. It would not be until six years later that I'd fully understand how that commitment to that mission trip would mark my life's path.

2 Timothy 2:19, *"God's solid foundation stands firm, sealed with this inscription: 'The Lord knows those who are his,' and, 'Everyone who confesses the name of the Lord must turn away from wickedness.'"*

After returning, I had a couple health scares that caused me to be on bed rest for months at a time. I initially hated the isolation of it, but I used the time to spend worshipping God. God was using this time of isolation as a time of maturing me. Just like the Painted Lady caterpillars I helped raise in first grade had to go through a cocoon process, the chrysalis that isolated them also became their protection. God was using this time to mature my soul, and to transform my mind, and my will, and my emotions into one that reflected His thinking. By putting on the "garment of praise" my depression lifted. As Isaiah 61 proclaims,

"The Spirit of the Lord GOD is upon Me,
Because the LORD has anointed Me
To preach good tidings to the poor;
He has sent Me to heal the brokenhearted,
To proclaim liberty to the captives,
And the opening of the prison to those who are bound;

To proclaim the acceptable year of the LORD, And the day of vengeance of our God;
To comfort all who mourn,

To console those who mourn in Zion,
To give them beauty for ashes,
The oil of joy for mourning,
The garment of praise for the spirit of heaviness;
That they may be called trees of righteousness,
The planting of the LORD, that He may be glorified."

My husband and I became intimate again, and I ended up getting pregnant. Even though our relationship was better, I was so mad when

I found out I was pregnant. Thoughts re-entered my mind that I didn't like, and I felt trapped in the marriage for sure now. Three months into the pregnancy, I began going into pre-term labor. The memories of having our first child born premature, and the heartache that accompanied that time flooded back. The doctor tried stopping the labor with medication, and eventually put me on full bed rest with only bathroom privileges. My world came to a halt! My son was three years old, basically caring for himself, while I lay in bed. My days were spent with most of the hours in worship with my son. God used that time to bond us and draw us closer to Him.

Despite a decrease in pay, my husband changed his work schedule, and began attending church consistently. When I was 36 weeks gestation, my doctor removed me from bed rest, and my husband and I attended a church service together. As we were leaving the service, our pastor stopped us in the parking lot. He knew about my previous infidelity, and he stopped, put his hand on my pregnant belly, and said, "You hold your head high here, you are a child of the Most High God." I began to weep, and then he prayed a prayer over us, that our marriage would be a testimony of God's mercy, and our child would be everything God called him to be. He even prayed we would pick the perfect name for our new son.

My feelings started to change for my husband. I began to see him as a real life example of what Christ did for me on the cross. Christ's forgiveness was represented in my own marriage. I had a man who forgave me just as Jesus did. It was a picture of Christ and the church. No matter how many times we turn our backs on Jesus, He is always quick to forgive when we are repentant. The amazing thing was my husband never talked about what I did. Even when we had disagreements, he never threw my sin in my face. How was this possible? If the situation was reversed, could I do the same?

My husband enrolled in the graduate program at the local university and worked faithfully at completing his master's degree. Even though he was busier than ever with work and school, it seemed like he had more time for me. It was amazing how when you follow God's priorities, time management becomes a reality instead of a goal.

I still had lots of thoughts about my ex. I would ask God to help me with those feelings and memories. I could see that my obsession and consistent thinking about him is what caused me to get in the situation I had gotten into. The Scriptures in Romans (Amplified version) came to mind that said,

I APPEAL to you therefore, brethren, and beg of you in view of [all] the mercies of God, to make a decisive dedication of your bodies [presenting all your members and faculties] as a living sacrifice, holy (devoted, consecrated) and well pleasing to God, which is your reasonable (rational, intelligent) service and spiritual worship.

*Do not be conformed to this world (this age), [fashioned after and adapted to its external, superficial customs], but be **transformed (changed)** by **the [entire] renewal of your mind** [by its new ideals and its new attitude], so that you may prove [for yourselves] what is the good and acceptable and perfect will of God, even the thing which is good and acceptable and perfect [in His sight for you].*

For by the grace (unmerited favor of God) given to me I warn everyone among you not to estimate and think of himself more highly than he ought [not to have an exaggerated opinion of his own importance], but to rate his ability with sober judgment, each according to the degree of faith apportioned by God to him. – Romans 12:1-3

STARTING FRESH

I understood that even though my spirit had been changed at conversion, my soul hadn't been saved. I had never renewed my mind (my soul) with the Word of God. My weekly church attendance, even my weekly Bible studies weren't doing enough to renew my mind. I committed to daily reading of the Scriptures, and consistent meditating on the verses that dealt with this issue. I also committed to speaking the Word over my life, out loud. This was awkward to do, but I knew that if *"faith comes by hearing and hearing by the Word of God,"* then hearing myself speak the Word would make my faith that much stronger!

When our second son was born healthy, things became better for our marriage. Our total family commitment to Christ was pure, intentional and dedicated. Even though I still fought battles of old thoughts and memories, the Word of God in my mouth became my anchor to control those thoughts. My soul was coming into alignment with my spirit. Ephesians 6 became my battle cry.

Finally, be strong in the Lord and in his mighty power. Put on the full armor of God, so that you can take your stand against the devil's schemes. For our struggle is not against flesh and blood, but against the rulers, against the authorities, against the powers of this dark world and against the spiritual forces of evil in the heavenly realms. Therefore **put on the full armor of God,** *so that when the day of evil comes, you may be able to stand your ground, and after you have done everything, to stand. Stand firm then, with the belt of truth buckled around your waist, with the breastplate of righteousness in place, and with your feet fitted with the readiness that comes from the gospel of peace. In addition to all this, take up the shield of faith, with which you can extinguish all the flaming arrows of the evil one. Take the helmet of salvation and the sword of the Spirit, which is the word of God. –* Ephesians 6:10-17

When our youngest was a year old, my husband completed his master's degree, and received a job offer in the area where we used to live. Memories of the loneliness and pain that existed when we lived there before were replaced with excitement and anticipation of a family moving to shine God's light. We were living completely for Him now. I told my husband that when we relocated, every decision and every choice I made will be to honor Christ and to obey Him. Whatever He wanted to do with my life, He could.

As soon as we moved, the Lord imprinted Deuteronomy 30 on my soul. In the Message paraphrase of verse 14 and following, it says,:

"The word is right here and now—as near as the tongue in your mouth, as near as the heart in your chest. **Just do it!** *Look at what I've done for you today: I've placed in front of you: Life and Good, Death and Evil. And I command you today: Love GOD, your God. Walk in his ways. Keep his commandments, regulations, and rules so that you will live, really live, live exuberantly, blessed by GOD, your God, in the land you are about to enter and possess."*

We moved from an area of low income dwellings to mid-upper income neighborhoods. I had never lived in an area like this before. There were perfectly manicured lawns, landscaped property, and moms who all stayed home with their young ones – everything here was different. It was beautiful, and God was blessing us with our home, but I felt out of place. My husband instantly gained local popularity as he now worked for the neighborhood pediatrics' office. Everyone wanted to friend me, and it was clear it wasn't so much for me, but so they'd have access to "after hours" healthcare if their child fell ill. Whatever the case, it didn't matter, God sent us here.

I began actively volunteering at my oldest son's elementary school. I grew up the daughter of a teacher, and a great student myself, but I had never seen volunteerism like this in a school. Not just an occasional home-room mom in attendance, but at least four mothers volunteering each school day, and that was just in the kindergarten/first grade area! More and more of these stay-at-home moms befriended me, especially when they found out who my husband was!

I knew how to minister to others who grew up like me. I was even comfortable talking with someone who lived on the streets, but upper class suburbia freaked me out! I heard God clearly speak to me. I don't like using that phrase – "God spoke to me," but He actually did. He told me I was going to have to befriend these other stay-at-home moms. He told me that He loved them just like He loves me, and He showed me that behind the perfect home, there was a deep pain. He told me to join the local moms-club. He also told me I was to have Bible studies in my home for them. Also, He instructed me to make it mom and kid-friendly – to make it so low-key and so relaxed that kids could run around and play, and infants could nurse during the Bible study. So I did. And they came. And many were saved, and many rededicated their lives back to Christ.

My family and I immediately immersed ourselves into church. We knew exactly where to attend church because we had lived near this area once before, just in a different type of community. I jumped into volunteering, and for the first time, so did my husband. This was so new to us because he had never had a work schedule that allowed for serving in the church, and now we were serving together. Each Sunday, as we approached the church property, I would pray, *"Jesus, you have something to teach me today. Burn it into my mind, imprint it on my heart. Let me turn around and re-teach it to others this week."* That was exactly what He did. He made the messages the pastor shared so clear to me, and I would take the notes I jotted down during service, and re-work them simply. Then, each week I would re-teach the message that was shared. Lives were being changed.

God started giving us great friends, some through the Bible studies, some through the church, and some in the neighborhood, and, in each case, God used us to speak life into their lives and into their marriages.

We began attending a couples' Sunday school class, and met lots of other couples. To be honest, I didn't really like the class all that much, but I liked the relationships we formed. It would be clear later that some of these relationships would impact future ministry.

THE CLEAR CALL

Grace defies reason and logic. Love interrupts, if you like, the consequences of your actions, which in my case is very good news indeed, because I've done a lot of stupid stuff. –Bono[5]

One morning in worship service, I had a vision. The pastor briefly mentioned a theology school that had a campus at our church, and he also mentioned a Paul Timothy Program. This program was for those who felt called into full time ministry in one of the fivefold ministry gifts. It was also for those called to become full time missionaries.

Ephesians 4:11-13, *"So Christ himself gave the apostles, the prophets, the evangelists, the pastors and teachers, to equip his people for works of service, so that the body of Christ may be built up until we all reach unity in the faith and in the knowledge of the Son of God and become mature, attaining to the whole measure of the fullness of Christ."*

As he spoke, it was as if a big hole ripped through the ceiling of the sanctuary, and a beam of the brightest sunlight shone through, and rested and burned on my face. I had this happen to me at age fourteen, prior to my rededication to the Lord, so I knew what this was! I knew the Lord was telling me to do this. When we got home, I told my husband. He was silent. His silence angered me at first because I KNEW God wanted me to do this. Yes, there was a tuition involved in this program and with these classes, and yes we had a huge student loan debt that we were battling. But when God speaks, whether it's through his Word or through the still small voice of the Holy Spirit or a weird spotlight from the sky, you MUST obey it. I was done playing games. I didn't argue with my husband, but I did tell him *I was going* to do this.

When I was filling out the application for the program there was a section that said, "How do you intend to pay for the tuition?" I wrote as my answer, "Jehovah Jireh." Jehovah Jireh means the Lord our Provider. He is the one who meets our needs according to His riches in glory.

Genesis 22:14 (KJV), *"And Abraham called the name of that place Jehovah Jireh: as it is said to this day, In the mount of the LORD it shall be seen."*

Honestly, I had no idea where the money for the tuition would come from, but it didn't matter. God was teaching me that my husband was not my provider. He was showing me that He has that role in my life. Whatever God was calling me to do; He will always provide what I need. In the book called, *Why Not Women?*, by Loren Cunningham and David Joel Hamilton, it states, "He would never ask you to do something without giving you the ability to accomplish it, nor would he give you a gift and then tell you never use it."[6]

God was calling me to be a pastor. This was definitely not something I wanted! Honestly, I didn't think I would qualify with my track record, and, to top it off, when I speak in front of people, I usually cry. But this is God we are talking about, the one who so freely forgave me, and washed me clean; He's the one that remembers my sin no more. I could not say no to Him. "To obey is better than sacrifice…" repeated over and over in my mind. Nothing would stop me from fulfilling my call.

In typical God fashion, He showed me a creative way to earn money in the few short hours my youngest was in preschool. I cleaned some of the big houses near me and banked some serious cash. Every time I would get paid, I would set aside my tithe (God's 10 percent talked about throughout the Bible), and I would take the remainder to my professor. Later, I was told that I was the only one in that Program (during those three years) who paid their tuition on time and in full. Praise be to the One who provides!

My husband and I ended up becoming leaders in the Couples Ministry as well as other parts of the church. We hosted a couple's small group in our home for almost seven years. There was one season where we hosted thirteen small groups or Bible studies in our home each month. That season was short lived, and God used a mentor to speak into my life about balance and priorities. I learned that even though I'm good at something, and even though lives are being changed, it doesn't make it the right thing to do. My husband and I quickly assessed and re-evaluated everything we were doing, and re-organized our schedules. Here we were ministering to couples and young families, but we weren't spending the time we needed to as a couple. The Book of James instructs us *to be quick to listen*, so we immediately corrected and readjusted our priorities (James 1:19).

Psalm 130: 23-24, (The Message), *Investigate my life, O God, find out everything about me; Cross-examine and test me, get a clear picture of what I'm about; See for yourself whether I've done anything wrong— then guide me on the road to eternal life.*

HIS VISION, his VISION

My husband took the plunge and got baptized one night. He had been a Christian since he was eighteen years old, but the Holy Spirit really dealt with Him on being obedient to all His commands. After his baptism, I saw an immediate change in him. He never had much passion about anything, just a go with the flow kind of guy, but overnight he became full of great zeal for the Lord!

Romans 12:10-11, *"Be devoted to one another in love. Honor one another above yourselves. Never be lacking in zeal, but keep your spiritual fervor, serving the Lord.*

This new fervor caused him to sign up for a mission trip to the Dominican Republic. Most of the team was from our church's Spanish fellowship, and my husband was one of three English speaking people on the entire team! He made some great new friends, and God used him on that trip. He came back completely changed and excited about missions. His speaking and teaching in our small groups became more powerful, and before you knew it, we were both signed up for the same trip the following year.

I was in the middle of my Paul Timothy Program, and had just earned my Bachelors in Theology, when we were preparing for our trip to the Dominican Republic. The leaders of the couples' ministry ended up being selected as the team trip leaders, so the trip evolved to be a couples-only trip. Several of our friends signed up, and we began having instructional meetings as the time approached for us to leave. We would practice sharing our personal testimonies or stories of God's faithfulness in front of the team in preparation. Most of these would be about how God changed our lives or a story of God's healing power in our lives. Then the lead pastor said we were going to host a marriage conference at one of the churches in the D.R. She said, "Next week each couple will get up in front of the group and share their marriage testimony." What? Our marriage testimony? I didn't want to do that! My husband and I never discussed what happened between us. Thanks to the Lord we were still together, and were now being used for His glory. But our testimony? I didn't want to talk about it. Things were working out great NOT talking about it!

So here we were, driving the half hour home from church, both shocked at our new instructions for the next week! My husband turned to me and said, "Well, we are going to have to talk about it." No Joke! But How? We didn't even know where to start. So we started practicing talking about it, and how we would even start this story. I began crying, and starting talking about what I did. Then, I said, "when I told you what I did, you punched a hole in the wall, and then said...'I'm going to forgive you!'" My husband said, "Did I say that? I don't remember saying that!" I said, "Yeah you did, and that made me so mad 'cause I didn't want forgiveness, I wanted freedom." So we continued talking and talking and crying, then my husband said something I never knew. He said, "Then God gave me that vision." What?! I never knew of a vision! I never really knew why he stayed with me. He began to explain to me that he cried out to God for the first time since his conversion. While he was crying out he saw a huge arena of people, and they were all on their knees in worship and in reverence. Jesus was on the center stage as the mass of people were on their knees before Him. Then Jesus looked up and made eye contact with my husband. He said, "*Do you know why these people are here?*" My husband shook his head as to say no. Jesus continued, "*They are all here because Shannon brought them to me."* At that moment the vision was over. I was bawling at that point, and my husband said, "that was how I was able to forgive you, because I now saw you how Jesus sees you, and I knew God was going to use you in this way."

I was blown away. I couldn't see because of the tears; I was sobbing so hard. The love Jesus has for me! The love my husband has for me...it was overwhelming! God gave me an earthly representation of Jesus' love and forgiveness in my own marriage! I now could see clearly. God wasn't just calling me for full time service; He was calling the both of us. Our conversation continued, and on the mission field in Santiago, Dominican Republic, we boldly shared our story through the help of an interpreter. At the end of that conference, the translator chased us down shouting, "Stop! Wait! This couple insists on talking to you!" Through the interpreter's help we found out that this couple came to the marriage conference as a last ditch effort. The wife said to me, "Your story is word for word the same as our story. Even the length of time you have been married, even the length of time of your relationship with your ex-boyfriend, even the reason for the affair...it's exactly the same!" The husband said that God had sent my husband and I here to speak directly to them, and because of our story, they now had hope in Jesus Christ to restore their marriage too!

Revelation 12:11 declares that *we overcome by the blood of the Lamb* ***AND*** *the word of our testimony!*

After that mission trip, God began to have my husband and I share parts of our testimony in our small group meetings and in our couples Sunday school class. Tears flowed each time as I knew I deliberately cheated on my husband so he'd leave me and I could be with my former love. My husband remained stoic as I spoke, and each time he would add how his lack of attention contributed to my choices. This would make me feel worse, and so undeserving of his love and forgiveness. Each time we shared our story, couples would come forward after we spoke, and would confess similar actions one of them made in their marriages. This would open the door for prayer and counseling, and God delivered His restoration to others just as freely as He gave it to us.

This couples' ministry continued for years. Every time we gave our testimony, I would feel like all the wind was knocked out of me. I would be physically exhausted from sharing such intimate details. But the raw emotions and the physical weakness couldn't hold a candle to the benefits of sharing our story. We saw many marriages stay together because of our transparency.

One day, I picked up a copy of the *Indiana Jones Trilogy* for my boys. We sat down to watch the series. As we put on the second movie, *Temple of Doom*[3], I immediately had to run out of the room. I could still hear the movie from my bedroom on the other end of the house, and strange flashes of what seemed to be memories came flooding back to my mind. I shut off the movie, but the images and feelings didn't stop. For months later, I continued to dream about that night, 20 years earlier. Were these memories real? I was still in occasional contact with my carefree friend from so long ago, so I reached out to her and asked her if she knew anything about that night. She confirmed that what I was remembering about her brother was accurate.

I would find myself crying for no reason; sometimes at work, sometimes while I was volunteering at church, sometimes in the car, sometimes in a meeting. It was uncontrollable and embarrassing, and every thought was on what he did to me. This happened so many years before. Why was I reacting to the memories like this? Then my thoughts would race to every sexual act I took part in after that moment.

I eventually received counseling from a female pastor who had been mentoring me at the time. Well, she sought me out as my torment was so obvious to her. She spent hours with me one morning, and she had me talk about every feeling I remembered about that time. I wept uncontrollably, and she spoke God's healing Scriptures over me. She said something I will never forget. She said, "How did you feel at that moment?" I said, "I felt like I was abandoned and alone." I had felt that

God had turned and looked away, and I was unprotected. She said, "Don't you see that every time after that moment in your life when you felt abandoned or lonely or unprotected, you made a sexual choice? You made a sexual choice every time you were lonely *because* one had been made for you." It was like it finally clicked for me. It was true! In the loneliest time in my marriage, I sought out the comfort of sex with the one who made me feel not alone.

NOT ON A TABLET OF STONE

My mind was becoming renewed not just by good, wise counsel, but by the constant washing of the Word. I had justified behaviors and choices for years, none which lined up with God's Word. None were in obedience to Him. Now, because of a repentant heart, He had cleansed me of my choices and sins that were against Him, but He was taking things a step further. I was now ready to be healed of things that had happened to me so long ago. Things that were buried for so long were now being dug up and exposed to Jesus' light. His Word is truly a *"lamp for my feet and a light on my path."*[7] Things had been blocked in my mind and in my memory for so long, and now God was bringing these things into the light and exposing them to His light and His love.

Hebrews 4:12-13 states, *"For the word of God is alive and active. Sharper than any double-edged sword, it penetrates even to dividing soul and spirit, joints and marrow; it judges the thoughts and attitudes of the heart. Nothing in all creation is hidden from God's sight. Everything is uncovered and laid bare before the eyes of him to whom we must give account."*

I had some friends in college who liked holding fancy dinner parties and progressive dinners. They would go to great lengths, and often great expense, to send formal invitations to their parties on fine, linen stationary with hot wax dripped onto the envelope and then a fleur de lis stamp pressed into the wax as a seal. Other than the fact I had some bizarre friends, I did enjoy getting the invitations in the mail. They were so formal, so special. I would have to take a knife to break the seal to get to the invitation itself. The invitation ink that was used was of high quality as well, and great effort was spent in the calligraphy font. It would make me think of the kings of old, and the decrees and letters that were sent from their authoritative hand by messenger.

The Old Testament speaks of kings who wrote letters, and before they sent them out they would seal them with their signet ring. If something was signed and sealed with the king's signet ring, the law or decree could not be revoked (i.e. Esther Chapter 8)

When God, the King of Kings, writes a letter, or leaves a mark, what type of ink does He use? Is it a dry erase marker so that, with a quick swipe, His writings can be removed? Is it like a henna tattoo that lasts somewhere between 17 and 30 days? Is it a Sharpie®? Can a Magic Eraser® be applied to His words so that they are easily removed? Of course not! *His words are lasting!* His words never come back empty! His ink is different. He uses the living Spirit of God to write His letters, and He uses our hearts to write them on!

2 Corinthians 3:1-3, *Are we beginning to commend ourselves again? Or do we need, like some people, letters of recommendation to you or from you? You yourselves are our letter, written on our hearts, known and read by everyone. You show that you are a letter from Christ, the result of our ministry, written not with ink but with the Spirit of the living God, not on tablets of stone but on tablets of human hearts.*

BIG UGLY BRUISES

The prophet Isaiah speaks of Jesus' crucifixion 800 years before the event ever took place.

In Isaiah 53:2-5 reads, *"He grew up before him like a tender shoot,*
and like a root out of dry ground.
He had no beauty or majesty to attract us to him,
nothing in his appearance that we should desire him.
He was despised and rejected by mankind,
a man of suffering, and familiar with pain.
Like one from whom people hide their faces
he was despised, and we held him in low esteem.

Surely he took up our pain
and bore our suffering,
yet we considered him punished by God,
stricken by him, and afflicted.

But he was pierced for our transgressions,
he was crushed for our iniquities;
the punishment that brought us peace was on him,
and by his wounds we are healed."

I often use the passage when preparing to pray for someone's healing, but honestly, there were times I didn't really understand the "iniquity" passage. I began to study out the topic. What is an iniquity? I've learned that an iniquity is a secret sin, like a sin you commit over and over without a consistent breakthrough in the deliverance from that sin. This is the type of sin spoken about by the apostle Paul in Romans 7: 15:

"I do not understand what I do. For what I want to do I do not do, but what I hate to do."

Everyone has dealt with some aspect of this type of sin. Some iniquities can include a consistent temptation to look at pornography, or maybe a constant crave for alcohol with no way to slow down, or a desire to be with someone sexually in a way that the Bible warns against. Sometimes an iniquity sticks around because of an unrepentant spirit, and sometimes because of a generational sin or curse. But for many, an iniquity can come from something that was done "to us." For instance, in my case, a sexual act was done to me. A pattern of sexual choices became a stronghold in my life, and therefore an iniquity I didn't know how to control. So, a person either does one of two things: they either justify the behavior or see it for what it really is in the reflection of the mirror of the Word of God, and deal with it.

2 Corinthians 10:3-5 tells us, *"For though we live in the world, we do not wage war as the world does. The weapons we fight with are not the weapons of the world. On the contrary, they have divine power to demolish strongholds. We demolish arguments and every pretension that sets itself up against the knowledge of God, and we take captive every thought to make it obedient to Christ."*

Not knowing how to deal with this, my brain just blocked it out of my memory for 20 years. Eventually, and through God's perfect timing, it was brought back to my memory, and it had to be dealt with. I was now mature enough in my faith in the Word, that I knew how to fight strongholds and take captive thoughts, and make them obedient to God.

The King James Version of the Isaiah verse say that Jesus was *bruised for our iniquities*. I was always getting bruises as a little girl. My sister and I were dancers, and we played hard outside with the neighbors - relay races, soccer and acrobatics, riding our bikes until the streetlights came on. All of these fun, neighborhood activities would eventually at some point cause someone, *usually me,* to have a big bruise somewhere on my body. Those bruises were ugly to look at, but they were also very tender to touch. Even the tiniest pressure would bring pain.

Someone told me that a bruise is an outside evidence of an inside bleeding. It is caused by underlying blood vessels that have ruptured. I got to thinking more about this. If the stripes on Jesus' back produced the cleansing blood to heal us of our diseases, then the bruises that caused an internal bleeding and tenderness to touch will heal us of our iniquities. There is power, wonder working power in the blood of Jesus. His blood is strong enough to wipe out every iniquity! Secret, sometimes shameful sins or habits are hidden by most, but they are never hidden to Jesus. His blood paid the price for the emotional hurts the same way it paid the price for the physical hurts.

I now saw the full healing power of the blood of Jesus for myself. His cleansing blood washed those inner hurts away. My pattern of wrong behaviors had been broken.

METAMORPHOSIS

God had performed a complete transformation in me. My spirit was transformed and made new at my conversion. But, now my soul – my mind, my will and my emotions were being restored. Just like a caterpillar enters the chrysalis stage, and transforms into a butterfly, God was doing the same for me. My transformation process would also end with wings that would allow me to soar on the wind of the breath of the Holy Spirit. Interestingly, the word for transformation is the same word for restoration. That word in the Greek language is "metamorphoo." Does that word look familiar? A metamorphosis is what happened to the caterpillar, like the Painted Ladies I watched transform in first grade. They went through a process, and came through with wings that could fly. We had to release them into nature. They no longer could stay in the container that the transformation took place in – the aquarium. They needed to spread their wings and soar.

This is the story of what happened to my husband and me. Major healing took place, in both our hearts. Those previous short term mission experiences were a launching pad for something far greater. The children's ministry I was involved with as a child and the visions I saw made sense now. We were ready to take our dedication and service to Him to another level. He was calling us to launch a ministry of our own. I had been employed at this point with a position of ministry in a large church, and I received a nice paycheck for my ministry work. In typical God fashion, He told us to do something completely different, and with no compensation. We took off soaring together into the great unknown when He specifically told us that I was to quit my job, and we were to start a home church and a missions organization of our own. We joined efforts with my father, and started taking teams on short term trips all over the world. We named the ministry after our youngest son, the one who was prayed over by our pastor to have the perfect name. Our kids join us in these pursuits to third world nations and to U.S. inner cities.

Jesus speaks to us in Acts 1:8:

"But you will receive power when the Holy Spirit comes on you; and you will be my witnesses in Jerusalem, and in all Judea and Samaria, and to the ends of the earth."

The Holy Spirit showed us that Jerusalem is our local area, Judea is our state, Samaria is our country, and the ends of the earth is just everywhere else. He wants to be strategic with our church, our outreaches, our missions; that is - hit each of these areas.   Since Jesus spoke these words before ascending into heaven, they must be pretty important!

This is what we immediately began doing, and we have seen great blessings take place because of the obedience to His voice.

TAKING BACK WHAT WAS STOLEN

In Matthew chapter 21 we find Jesus about to embark on the final week of his earthly life.

As they approached Jerusalem and came to Bethpage on the Mount of Olives, Jesus sent two disciples saying to them, "Go to the village ahead of you, and at once you will find a donkey tied there, with her colt by her. Untie them and bring them to me. If anyone says anything to you, say that the Lord needs them, and he will send them right away." – Matthew 21:1-3

Jesus leaves the safety and security of ministry, and His life is about to be changed forever.

I often think about some of the choices I've made – leaving security and comfort behind for the sake of something greater – something that requires obedience – something of eternal worth. It's never easy, and it usually comes at a high price. That subject of "opportunity cost" that's taught so extensively in college really comes into play. What do we have to give up in order to obey the greater voice?

This is a story about those choices – *the ones of value* – not value as Americans and the financially affluent would know it, but a lasting reward – a reward that won't be known until we are "caught up together with them in the clouds to meet the Lord in the air"[8]

When Jesus rode into the Holy City on that donkey, and the world finally recognized Him as the King of Kings, they got out their versions of the flag – the palm branches – and began to wave them proudly at the One who was about to change lives forever.

The crowd shouted "Hosanna... Hosanna,"[9] which means "Save Us." They were not only recognizing Jesus as King, but they were honoring Him as the One who would rescue them and make something beautiful out their mess. His decisions during this "passion week" would allow them – us – to become "sons and daughters"[10] of the Most High God.

"Behold what manner of love the Father has given unto us. That we might be called the sons of God."- 1 John 3:1

After Jesus' grand, yet strangely humble entrance into Jerusalem, He immediately went to His Father's house, the Temple. What He found there appalled Him. Crooks, money changers - a complete marketplace had taken over that sacred temple.

Jesus entered the temple courts and drove out all who were buying and selling there. He overturned the tables of the money changers and the benches of those selling doves. "It is written," he said to them, "'My house will be called a house of prayer, but you are making it 'a den of robbers.'"- Matthew 21:12-13

I often reflect on how we are referred to in Scripture as the *"temple of the Holy Spirit"*[11] – how our bodies are meant to be sacred and holy and set apart for His service. Many times that is not the case, even for the proclaimed Christ-followers. We often turn our "temples" into marketplaces of sin and corruption. We even behave as the culture of the day behaves, and start justifying our feelings and actions as appropriate, when they are far from temple behavior. And then there are times where others, through no fault of our own, make those decisions for us, and they "defile" our temples. Through abuse or rape or any number of mistreatments, what was meant to be holy becomes a complete mess.

The assault against me when I was fourteen was not something I chose for myself. It did leave a scar on me though. It marked me as unclean, as tainted, as someone who isn't valuable. Of course, I know now that that is not at all how God sees me, but at the time that is the reflection I saw. That wrong perspective of myself altered my decision making process for years to come.

Jesus got angry as the Scriptures tell us in Matthew chapter 21. He made a whip, and he drove out those who turned God's house into a "den of robbers."

Have you turned your temple into a den of robbers? Have you believed a lie about yourself? Have you settled for less than God's perfect plan for your life and your body? Or worse yet, have others defiled you?

Jesus made quite a statement with those who defiled the Father's house. The Bible tells us He turned over the tables of the money changers. Imagine that! The aggression – the righteous anger – the force He used to clean that temple!

Yet that is exactly what He wants to do for you. He wants to turn the tables over on the enemy. He wants to flip them inside out and upside down! He wants your thinking to match His thinking. He wants to clean your temple, your body, even your soul. He took action, violent action! The Word of God states that "the violent take it by force."[12] It also says that "faith, if it hath not works, is dead".[13]

If the great Creator of the Universe took this sort of action, shouldn't we as Christ-followers follow His lead? Because of what Jesus did for us on the cross, we were given the same authority and power as He has. We are called His co-heirs with Christ Jesus. So, in essence, everything that belongs to Jesus belongs to His followers. Everything that He did, we can do, and should do as imitators of Him. What a concept! We have that *same authority* to take back what was stolen. There's a verse I read that says He'll give you a double recompense for your distress[14].

Basically that means He will give you double for the trouble you had in your past.

After Jesus cleared the temple there is a verse that doesn't get much attention in the story, but it is my personal favorite. It says, *the blind and the lame came to him at the temple, and he healed them*[15]. Because he cleared out the enemy, the sick had access to Jesus, and they were healed. Amazing!

We have the same authority Jesus has to drive out the enemy who has tried to set up house in us. By the power of the Name above every Name, **the Name of Jesus**, we can command the defilement to leave.

Remember the charge given to us in the Great Commission?

*And these signs will accompany those who believe: In my name **they will drive out demons**; they will speak in new tongues; they will pick up snakes with their hands; and when they drink deadly poison, it will not hurt them at all; they will place their hands on sick people, and they will get well.* – Mark 16:17-18

These are not just signs for full time missionaries or pastors or even the most famous evangelist. Jesus said these things are signs that accompany "believers" - you and I, followers of Jesus, the Anointed One. That very same anointing that Jesus possesses, you and I have. It's resting on us. If you don't use it, and take action, violent force, you will never see results. It's like having a car, and having keys to the car. If you never take the keys, and start the engine, and drive, you will never go anywhere.

The salvation we initially received at our conversion literally means wholeness, soundness and completeness. Receive the full gift He has for you! It was only *after* the temple was cleared that the healings took place. All that junk and disgrace that blocks access to the Lord must go.

It's interesting to me that when the Word speaks of dwelling *"in the secret place of the Most High"* (Psalm 91:1) in that well known chapter on protection; it says that those who dwell there *"abide under the shadow of the Almighty."* To abide means to make your home with someone. In this case, if we make our home with the Lord, He makes His home with us, and we are in His presence at that point. Abiding with the Lord ensures us protection, safety, and a long life. That's what we want, right? We want to be able to really be with the Lord. That's what these people in Jerusalem wanted. They wanted access to a loving Savior who wanted nothing more than to heal what hurt them. Most times that hurt isn't a physical pain, but it's an emotional hurt - that kind of hurt that stays with a person for years and years, sometimes for decades, sometimes for a lifetime. It's the kind that damages a soul – a person's mind, will and emotions. Jesus came to heal that kind of pain.

The prophet Isaiah (Chapter 6) describes in detail what the Lord looks like. It speaks of God's robe, and the train of his robe filling *the whole temple*. I remember watching the wedding of Princess Di and Prince Charles when I was a young girl. Her wedding gown had a train that was 25 feet in length. It was the type of dress that commanded attention as she entered the Westminster Abbey. It got my attention! In contrast the train on the Lord's robe *FILLS* the entire temple! Remember that you are that temple, and when he takes up residence in you, He *FILLS* you to capacity. There is no room for anything else. He cleared the enemy out, and He moves in. He marks you as His own.

There's a worship song I love to sing called, *You Won't Relent.* The powerful lyrics are taken from the Song of Solomon. The song speaks of the Lord never giving up on having all of you, and His seal protecting His love from washing away. *"I'll set you as a seal upon my heart, As a seal upon my arm…Many waters cannot quench this love."*[16] His love for you is real. He never gives up on you. He will take all those scars, those imprints of pain, and press them in the palm of His mighty hand, and place a seal on you that will last forever! Allow Him to bring healing and restoration to your soul.

Song of Solomon 8:6-7, *"Place me like a seal over your heart, like a seal on your arm; for love is as strong as death, its jealousy unyielding as the grave. It burns like a blazing fire, like a mighty flame. Many waters cannot quench love; rivers cannot wash it away."*

This is what He wants for you. He wants to heal your deepest wounds and scars. He wants to seal your restored heart, and once it's sealed nothing can wash away His love for you! Will you make this moment a defining moment in your life? Will you ask Him to fill you? Will you ask Him to mark you and seal you?

SIGNED.

SEALED.

DELIVERED.

PRAYER OF SALVATION

Dear God. Thank you for loving me. Thank you for the chance to have a personal and intimate relationship with you. Lord, please forgive me for my sins. I know I have hurt you. I confess my need for you. I acknowledge that you died for my sins and I thank you. I realize I am a sinner and that I need your forgiveness. Thank you for forgiving me. And in the same way that you forgive me, right now I forgive all those who have hurt me, used me, or abused me [call out those names right now]. Help me also to forgive myself. Lord lead me to a church where I can learn more about the Bible and meet authentic people who are trying to grow like I am. Help me to read my Bible and spend time with you daily. Thank you for loving me. I will do my best to serve you in the best way I know how – trusting that you will teach me.

In Jesus' name. Amen!

If you prayed this prayer please contact the author:
spope@lifeinactionmission.com

She would love to help you as you start this journey!

END NOTES

1. John, Elton & Taupin, Bernie. "Daniel". <u>Don't Shoot Me I'm Only the Piano Player</u>. MCA, 1973.
2. Point of Grace. "Heal the Wound". <u>How You Live</u>. Word Entertainment, 2008.
3. *Indiana Jones and the Temple of Doom*. Dir. Steven Spielberg. 1984. Film.
4. Green, Keith. "To Obey is Better Than Sacrifice". <u>No Compromise</u>. Sparrow Records, 1978.
5. Cunningham, Loren, and David J. Hamilton. *Why Not Women?: A Fresh Look at Scripture on Women in Missions, Ministry, and Leadership*. Seattle, WA: YWAM Pub., 2000. Print.
6. Bono, and Michka Assayas. *Bono: In Conversation with Michka Assayas with a Foreword by Bono.* London: Hodder & Stoughton, 2005. Print
7. Psalm 119:105
8. 1 Thessalonians 4:17
9. Matthew 21:9
10. 2 Corinthians 6:18
11. 1 Corinthians 6:19
12. Matthew 11:12 (KJV)
13. James 2:17 (KJV)
14. Isaiah 61:7 (Ampliphied)
15. Matthew 21:14
16. Jesus Culture. "You Won't Relent". <u>Your Love Never Fails</u>. Kingsway Music, 2010.

ABOUT THE AUTHOR

Shannon Pope is the President of LIAM (a.k.a. Life In Action Mission) a non-profit 501(c)3 charity with campuses in the state of Missouri and the State of Florida. Shannon is a graduate of the University of Missouri-Columbia where she pursued a career in hospitality management. Her pursuits shifted into a different form of hospitality, serving God's people through a pastoral calling with a strong emphasis in missions and humanitarian aid work, while earning a Master in Theology and a Master in Divinity. She specializes in mobilizing teams and volunteers to make a difference in today's society.

Shannon has a passion for not only helping the neighbor next door, but for reaching those without hope across the globe. She has led hundreds of community service outreaches in U.S. inner cities and impoverished neighborhoods. She also has orchestrated numerous foreign short-term mission trips with her family by her side and has led teams impacting today's third world countries. Justice issues and serving the brokenhearted are what drive this LIAM pastor. Shannon specializes in showing others how to live out the words and commands of Jesus. Her heart beats to show others how to become the Salt (modeling the truth) and the Light (teaching it to others) that the Lord Jesus taught in the famous Sermon on the Mount.

Shannon grew up in north county St. Louis and graduated from *Grace Christian High School*. She has a B.S. in Hotel and Restaurant Management from the *University of Missouri- Columbia*. She also earned her Bachelor in Theology, Master of Theology and a Master of Divinity from *Christian Life School of Theology*. She currently pastors a house church, and resides with her two sons and husband of eighteen years in Tampa, Florida.

Pastor Shannon is available to speak at conferences and churches. Please contact her through the website, www.lifeinactionmission.com

NOTES

NOTES

NOTES

NOTES

NOTES

NOTES

Made in the USA
Charleston, SC
10 August 2012